BICYCLE TOURING
THE
CANADIAN
GULF ISLANDS

by
Stelle Enloe
and
Byron A. Richardson

Printed in the United States of America

First Printing 1985

© Copyright by BAR Co.
1900 Westlake Avenue North
Seattle, Washington 98109

ISBN 0-9615482-0-7

Dedicated to the memory of Barbara Savage, author of *Miles From Nowhere*

Contents

ntroduction

AREA MAP

VANCOUVER

TSAWWASSEN

STRAIT OF GEORGIA

NORTH

SATURNA

SATURNA ISLAND

PLUMPER SOUND

STURDIES BAY

MAYNE ISLAND

ACTIVE

VILLAGE BAY

PENDER ISLANDS

GALIANO ISLAND

MONTAGUE HARBOR

LONG HARBOR

OTTER BAY

VESUVIUS

SALTSPRING ISLAND

FULFORD HARBOR

THETIS ISLAND

KUPER ISLAND

CROFTON

STUART ISLAND

JOHNS ISLAND

SPIEDEN ISLAND

SAN JUAN ISLAND

HENRY ISLAND

SIDNEY ISLAND

JAMES ISLAND

BAY

SIDNEY

VANCOUVER ISLAND

VICTORIA

Introduction

Several years ago we began to explore the Canadian Gulf Islands by bicycle. Touring the Gulf Islands on a bicycle provides one with an opportunity to view some of Canada's most magnificent scenery, to meet many of the islands' friendly residents, to enjoy sheltered beaches and to dine in unique restaurants. The exhilaration of discovering a new area, offering a sense of isolation and little traffic, has inspired us to share our adventures with you.

Bicycling offers the cyclist rewards which the motorist will never experience. On your bicycle you'll feel a sense of freedom and quiet serenity, and enjoy a comradeship with the other bikers you meet on the road, at the rest stops, and in the campsites. As you pedal along you will experience the sounds of nature, the fragrance of the trees, flowers and, yes, even the farm animals, the feel of the road beneath your bicycle, the wind in your face, the flushing out of deer, pheasants and the other wild animals you may suddenly come upon, and the sweat running down your brow. In addition, you will experience mental relaxation and the feeling that you are completely self-sufficient and at one with nature.

You will find that you are continually establishing personal challenges for yourself—distances to be traveled, hills to be climbed and destinations to be reached by specific times to meet those ferry schedules. In the process you will enjoy yourself and receive the satisfaction that comes from the attainment of personal goals. Your reward will be a good hot shower at the end of the day or a refreshing dip in the ocean or a lake.

Bicycle touring and camping, like mountaineering, can be very enjoyable provided you are adequately prepared and know what you are doing. If you are not prepared, it can be a miserable experience. Take the time before you venture forth on your Canadian Gulf Islands adventure to do a little planning. You will be amply rewarded.

Happy biking!

GULF ISLANDS

TO TSAWWASSEN B.C.

NORTH

STRAIT OF GEORGIA

STURDIES BAY

MONTAGUE HARBOR

GALIANO ISLAND

TRINCOMALI CHANNEL

LONG

VESUVIUS

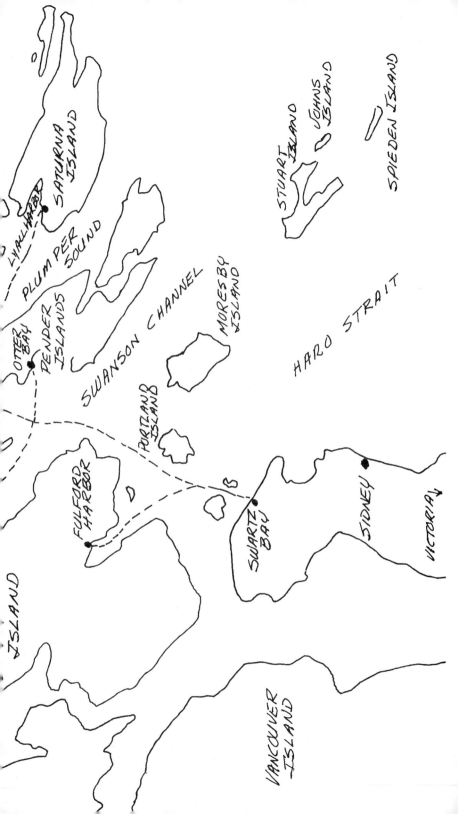

The Gulf Islands

Location

The Canadian Gulf Islands are located between Vancouver Island and British Columbia's lower mainland—about 100 statute air miles northwest of Seattle, Washington. Some 200 of these enchanting islands are clustered on the leeward side of Vancouver Island.

The populated islands—Saltspring, North and South Pender, Galiano, Mayne, and Saturna—are accessible by British Columbia ferries. The other islands are for the most part uninhabited and accessible only by private boat, canoe, or seaplane.

Today, over 7,000 permanent residents live in the islands. More than one-third of the Gulf Islands' permanent residents are over 55 years of age. Many of them are retired.

Getting There

South of Vancouver, Canada's Tsawwassen ferry connects the mainland to the Gulf Islands. Tsawwassen is approximately 140 freeway miles north of Seattle, Washington. Traveling at 70-75 mph (we are always late and the ferry doesn't wait), the journey takes approximately 2¼ hours, provided you are fortunate enough not to have encountered a friendly Washington State patrolman and have also had a very short wait for customs clearance at the Canadian border. Exit the freeway at the No. 10 exit, Ladner Tsawwassen Victoria Ferry. This allows approximately 10 short minutes to park the car at the Tsawwassen terminal, unload the car, load the gear on the bicycles, ride the short distance to the entrance gate, buy your tickets and make a mad dash to board

the ferry. Three hours' travel time is more realistic and is highly recommended.

You will enjoy the Canadian ferries. They are large, well equipped and very comfortable. The scenic run between Tsawwassen and Long Harbor on Saltspring Island varies in length from 1¾ hours to 2¾ hours, depending upon the route taken and the departure time. Ferry schedules may be obtained from the British Columbia Ferry Corporation, 2701 Alaskan Way, Pier 69 (Phone: (206) 682-6865) in Seattle. It is suggested that you call the terminal to insure that you have interpreted the schedule correctly prior to leaving, as the schedules can be confusing. It is a *long* wait between ferries in the event you miss your scheduled ferry. A word of caution: Should you take your car during the busy summer months, car reservations are recommended. For vehicle reservations, call the B.C. Ferries:

Vancouver: (604) 669-1211
Victoria: (604) 386-3431
Saltspring Island: (604) 537-9921
Outer Gulf Islands: (604) 629-3215

Accommodations and Campgrounds

For the bike camper, there are provincial parks with pit toilets throughout the islands, as well as commercial campgrounds for those who prefer private camping. You should make your arrangements for overnight accommodations as early in the day as possible, as camping facilities are limited. *There are no overnight camping facilities for bikers or hikers on Mayne Island or on Saturna Island.*

Should you find yourself marooned, there are resorts, hotels, lodges and bed-and-breakfast facilities on all of the islands. A late arriver may also find those facilities full. If that happens, keep a stiff upper lip—you will survive—we did!

SALTSPRING ISLAND

NORTH

SOUTHEY PT.

NORTH END RD.

SUNSET DR.

ST. MARY LAKE

VESUVIUS

VESUVIUS BAY RD.

UPPER GANGES RD.

LOWER GANGES RD.

GANGES

GANGES

LONG HARBOR RD.

LONG HARBOR

GANGES

BOOTH BAY

FERRY TO CROFTON

FERRY TO VANCOUVER & OUTER ISLANDS

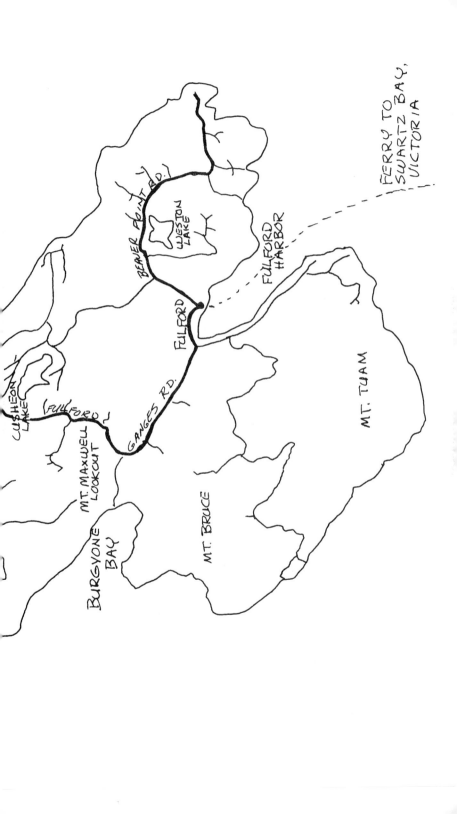

Saltspring Island

Distance: 83 miles
Terrain: Moderate to hilly, with several *steep* hills

Saltspring Island is the largest and most heavily populated of the Gulf Islands. The island is 69 square miles in size and is the home of over 6,000 people.

The island stretches approximately 18 miles from end to end and varies in width from 2 miles to 10 miles. More than 500 miles of winding roads offer visitors an opportunity to traverse this remarkably diverse island. The island has mountain peaks reaching 2,100 feet and presents breathtaking views, harbors, beaches and beautiful parks.

The island's roads, both paved and gravel, wind past lakes, farms, streams and wooded areas, and dip up and down numerous hills. The ocean, other islands, and mountains of mainland Canada and the United States can be glimpsed frequently from most of the roads on the island. More than likely, you will also encounter stray deer, sheep, or cows on the road.

Saltspring became the first of the Gulf Islands to be settled, in 1857. The island was originally named Chuam Island and later the name was changed to Admiral Island. Because there are natural salt springs located at the island's northern end, the name Saltspring persisted in spite of the recorded names the island was given. Most of the harbors, peaks and villages on Saltspring are named after British ships that charted the area.

Today, the island is served by three entry ports—Long Harbor, Fulford Harbor, and Vesuvius Bay. The Tsawwassen ferry sails across the Strait of Georgia into Sturdies Bay on Galiano Island, through beautiful Active Pass and into Village Bay on Mayne Island. From Village Bay, the ferry sails into

Otter Bay on Pender Island and then to Saltspring's Long Harbor. Each time we make this sailing, we are awed by the magnificent beauty of the rugged islands. The 2¾-hour trip will provide many picture-taking opportunities.

Fulford Harbor at Saltspring's south end links the island with Swartz Bay, which is the Victoria ferry terminal. The Swartz Bay ferry trip takes approximately half an hour and operates continuously each day.

The ferry from Vesuvius Bay on Saltspring to Crofton on Vancouver Island takes about 20 minutes to cross Stewart Channel.

Saltspring's main settlement, the unincorporated village of Ganges, sits at the apex of Ganges Harbor and is the center of activity on the island. We found Ganges to be a charming

and friendly village with interesting restaurants and fun shops. You will want to spend some time browsing around Mouat's General Store, which is housed in an old restored building displaying many fascinating pictures and artifacts from the early days in Ganges and Saltspring. It's a great place to check out the arts and crafts shops or have lunch in the little sandwich shop. You may want to take your lunch out on the bench and watch the activities in the harbor. Don't forget the ice cream store next door. If you have the time, plan on joining the local fair, held on Saturdays at the town park. The Tourist Information Center is located in downtown Ganges between Kanaka Place and Rita's Inn.

The community of Fernwood, about five miles north of Ganges, is the area where the island's first store was built, in 1859, by an Englishman, Jonathan Begg. In its original days, the community was known as Beggs Settlement and

became a meeting place for farmers at the north end of the island. Begg was known as a character, and if someone didn't like the way he ran his store, he would tell them to shop elsewhere. His customers had little choice but to conform to his stringent rules because there was nowhere else to shop on Saltspring Island. Today, the community of Fernwood has a small grocery store and gas station, a long pier and a government wharf which stretches into Trincomali Channel, as well a a new school.

At Vesuvius Bay, there is a small general store, a shop, restaurants and a pub. Vesuvius is also the terminal for the ferry to Crofton on Vancouver Island.

Fulford, at the head of Fulford Harbor, has a restaurant, small grocery store, gas station, and a pub. The ferry terminal marks the end of the line for the Vancouver Island ferry from Swartz Bay.

Ruckel Provincial Park, at Beaver Point, is the largest provincial park in the entire Gulf Islands. The park is located at the end of Beaver Point Road and is reached directly from the ferry wharf at Fulford Harbor. The park is an open camping area where you may pitch your tent, build a beach fire and watch the ferries as they frequently pass a hundred yards or so off Beaver Point—a truly beautiful sight, especially on a warm, clear summer evening. Water is available from a well pump near the park entrance, a fair distance from the campsite, so bring a large water container.

Mount Maxwell Provincial Park provides a spectacular view of Fulford Harbor, Burgoyne Bay and Vancouver Island. The park also has hiking trails offering breathtaking views. Mount Maxwell Park is reached via Cranberry Road, leading off to the west at the top of Ganges Hill. The road is very steep. The last portion is gravel and very rough. Not too bad, though, if you have a four-wheel-drive truck. Even then, you might get stuck. There are no overnight facilities for camping at the park, but the view is well worth the hike.

Mouat Provincial Park, in Ganges, is very small and often full. The park is reached from the foot of Ganges Hill off Seaview Avenue.

On the shores of St. Mary Lake, the largest of the island's lakes, are many resorts offering a variety of commercial camping facilities with swimming.

Accommodations

*A licensed facility serves alcoholic beverages.

Arbutus Court Motel, on Vesuvius Bay Road in Vesuvius, has 12 units, several with kitchens. Phone: (604) 537-5415.

Bed & Breakfasts:

A. R. Bryan Smith, North End Road, (604) 537-9362.
L'Ocean et Les Pins, 720 Beddis Road, (604) 537-9373.
Meg Hodges, 115 Forest Hills Place, (604) 537-4176.
W. O. & V. W. Davies, 231 Kings Lane, (604) 537-9839.
Ye Olde Devon Lodge, Lower Ganges Road, (604) 537-4288.

Booth Bay Resort, on Baker Road at Booth Bay, has quaint, secluded, fully equipped cottages overlooking the bay. The Bay Window Restaurant is located in an old lodge which is part of the resort. Phone: (604) 537-5651.

Blue Gables Family Resort & Campsite, at St. Mary Lake, has housekeeping cottages, camping facilities, showers, and a small store. Phone: (604) 537-5773.

Cedar Beach Resort, at St. Mary Lake, is a family vacation spot with a heated pool, sauna and a recreation room. Phone: (604) 537-2205.

Cusheon Lake Resort, on Natalie Road, has houskeeping cabins, swimming, boating and a hot tub. Phone: (604) 537-9629.

Fulford Inn, * at Fulford Harbor, has cozy rooms, a licensed dining room and pub. Phone: (604) 653-4432.

Green Acres Resort, on St. Mary Lake off Lang Road, has fully furnished, modern cottages. Phone: (604) 537-2585.

Harbor House Hotel, * in Ganges, is a modern hotel with a licensed dining room, lounge, pub and convention facilities. Phone: (604) 537-5571.

Hastings House, on the Upper Ganges Road, offers luxurious holiday living in a pastoral setting. Phone: (604) 537-2362.

Maple Ridge Resort, on St. Mary Lake, has kitchenette cottages. Phone: (604) 537-2311.

Rita's Inn, * in Ganges, provides quaint, comfortable room, community bathrooms, home cooked meals and a licensed dining room. A good place to stay should you need to take a late evening ferry. Phone: (604) 537-5338.

Seabreeze Motel, two blocks from Ganges, has one-bedroom units and some kitchenettes. Phone: (604) 537-4145.

Shady Willows Resort, on the west side of St. Mary Lake, has self-contained units, campsites, showers and flush toilets.

Spindrift Resort, by the ocean in Ganges, offers ocean-front cabins on a scenic peninsula. Phone: (604) 537-5311.

St. Mary Lake Resort, off North End Road, has fully equipped cabins, some with fireplaces. Phone: (604) 537-2832.

The Cottage Resort, off North End Road, offers self-contained housekeeping cottages. Phone: (604) 537-2214.

The Last Resort provides a secluded ocean view from self-contained cabins. Phone: (604) 537-4111.

Campgrounds

Mouat Provincial Park, at the base of the Ganges hill off Beaver Point Road, is a small provincial park with 15 campsites, pit toilets and well water.

Ruckel Provincial Park is located at the end of Beaver Point Road. The park is the largest provincial park in the islands and affords the camper ample tent sites on a large grassy field by the ocean, with commanding views of the ferries as they pass by Beaver Point.

NORTH SALTSPRING

NORTH

SOUTHEY PT.

NORTH END ROAD

NORTH BEACH RD.

NORTH END ROAD

SUNSET DRIVE

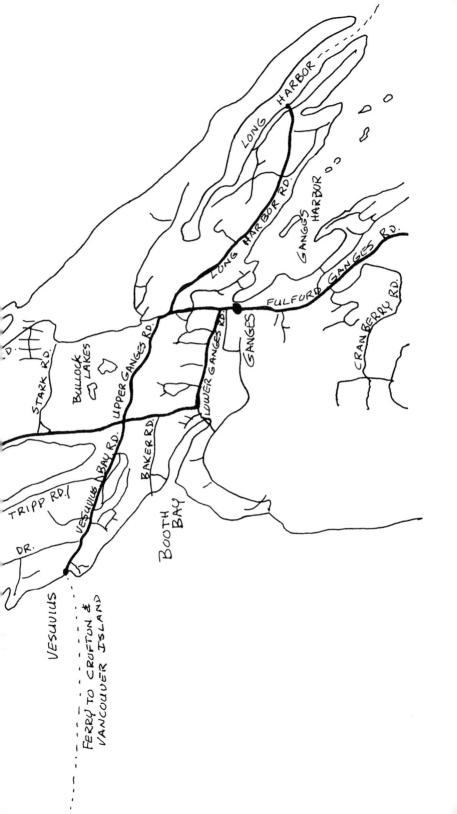

Your Route

North Saltspring—43 miles
Terrain: Moderate to hilly

0.0	Long Harbor Ferry Terminal—**straight ahead**
0.3	Entrance to Spindrift Resort on left (0.5 mile gravel road)
2.9	Junction—Long Harbor Road and Upper Ganges Road—**bear left**
3.4	Junction Lower Ganges Road—**go left** into Ganges
3.7	Rita's Inn on right
3.8	Ganges. Leaving Ganges to the north
4.1	Junction—Lower Ganges Road and Upper Ganges Road—**bear left** on Lower Ganges Road
6.8	Baker Road—**turn left** at cemetery
7.9	Booth Bay
9.0	Back to Lower Ganges road—**turn left**
9.3	Theatre and junction of Lower Ganges Road, Upper Ganges Road, North End Road and Vesuvius Bay Road—**turn left** onto Vesuvius Bay Road
9.9	Tripp Road on right—**turn right** and go up Tripp Road
10.3	Shady Willows
10.7	Maple Ridge Resort (gravel road)
11.4	End of road
12.8	Junction Tripp Road and Vesuvius Bay Road—**turn right**

14.1	Sunset Drive—continue straight ahead into Vesuvius (seaside kitchen, Inn at Vesuvius, Crofton Ferry and general store)
18.6	Southly Point Road—**turn left**
19.1	Junction—**bear right, then left**
19.6	End of road
20.1	Junction—**bear right**
20.6	End of road—beautiful sheltered bay
21.6	Back to Southly Point Road and Sunset Drive
23.2	Junction—North Beach Road and North End Road—**left** on North Beach Road
25.1	Fernwood Road on right—small store and boat dock—**straight ahead**
28.1	Walkers Hook Road, Robinson Road and Stark Road—continue on Robinson Road—steep hill
29.4	Robinson Road and Upper Ganges Road—**turn right**
30.9	Junction—Upper Ganges Road, Vesuvius Bay Road and North End Road (theatre)—**turn right** on North End Road
31.3	The Cottage Resort
32.1	Cedar Beach Resort
32.4	St. Mary Lake Resort
33.3	Blue Gables Resort
33.5	**Left** on Lang Road to lakeshore camping and R.V. park
34.0	Green Acres Resort
34.5	End of Lang Road
35.4	Back to North End Road
42.9	Rita's Inn

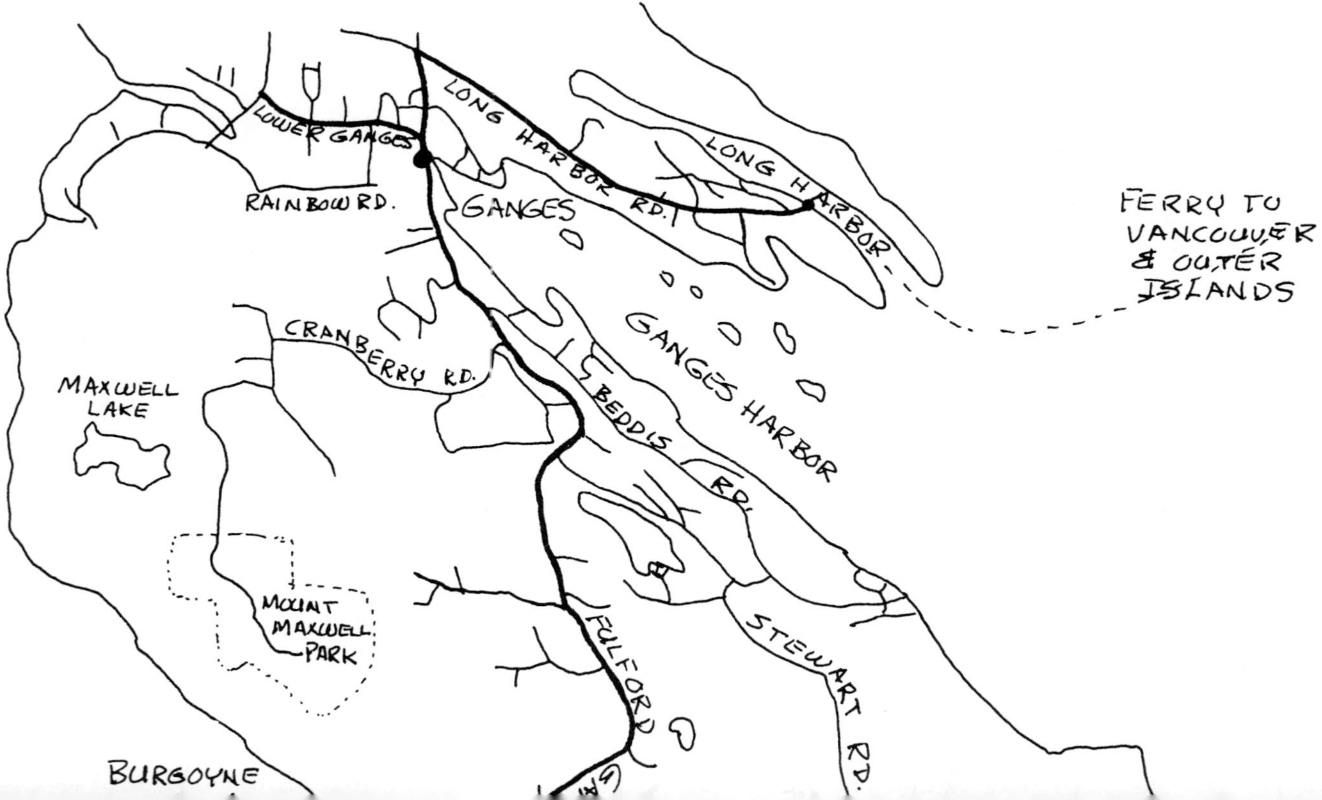

FERRY TO VANCOUVER & OUTER ISLANDS

LONG HARBOR

GANGES HARBOR

STEWART RD.

BEDDIS RD.

FULFORD

LONG HARBOR RD.

GANGES

LOWER GANGES

RAINBOW RD.

CRANBERRY RD.

MOUNT MAXWELL PARK

MAXWELL LAKE

BURGOYNE

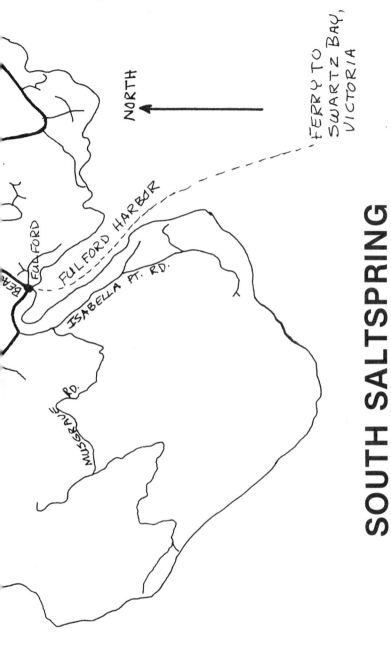

NORTH

FERRY TO SWARTZ BAY, VICTORIA

FULFORD HARBOR

FULFORD

BEA...

ISABELLA PT. RD.

MUSGRAVE RD.

SOUTH SALTSPRING

Your Route

South Saltspring—40 miles
Terrain: Hilly, with several *steep* hills

0.0   Centennial Park in downtown Ganges—
       proceed south up the steep hill on the
       Fulford Ganges Road

0.3   Mouat Provincial Park at end of Seaview
       Avenue

0.6   Back to Fulford Ganges Road—**turn right**

1.1   Left on Beddis Road—very picturesque

4.3   Intersection of Cusheon Lake Road (0.9
       miles on rough gravel road to Peter Park;
       scenic park with pit toilets but not recom-
       mended for bikers)

5.7   End of Beddis Road

10.3   Back to Fulford Ganges Road—**turn left**

11.1   Cranberry Road on right (5.5 miles to top
       of Mount Maxwell and park; gravel road
       begins in 2.5 miles on Cranberry Road.
       Good hike; not recommended for bicycles
       as road is *very* rough and steep)—
       continue **straight ahead** on Fulford
       Ganges Road

16.5   Fulford Inn

17.3   Fulford ferry dock—grocery store, Nan's
       Ice Cream Cones, and take-out restaurant

19.1   Stuart Road on left (2.2 miles of hilly
       gravel road leading to Cusheon Lake
       Road; not recommended)—**continue ahead**
       on Beaver Point Road

23.2	Entrance to Ruckel Provincial Park at Beaver Point
24.9	Returning to Ganges; Bridgeman Road on left (gravel—1.25 miles to end of road)
27.3	Stuart Road on right
29.9	Fulford Inn and Isabella Point Road (4.3 miles to end of Isabella Point Road and Hart Maxam Park)—**continue ahead** towards Ganges
31.9	Burgoyne Bay Road on the left—1.2 mile gravel road leading to Burgoyne Bay
33.1	Burgoyne Bay
34.3	Fulford Ganges Road—**turn left**
40.3	Ganges

PENDER ISLANDS

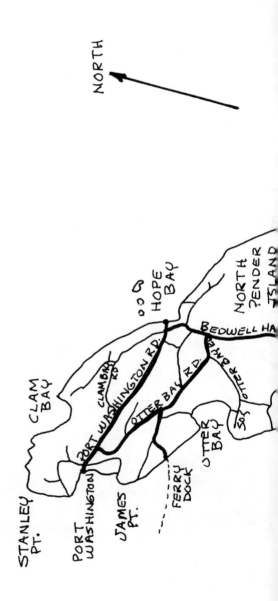

NORTH

STANLEY PT.

CLAM BAY

PORT WASHINGTON

PORT WASHINGTON RD.

CLAM BAY RD.

HOPE BAY

JAMES PT.

FERRY DOCK

OTTER BAY RD.

OTTER BAY

BEDWELL HA

OTTER

NORTH PENDER ISLAND

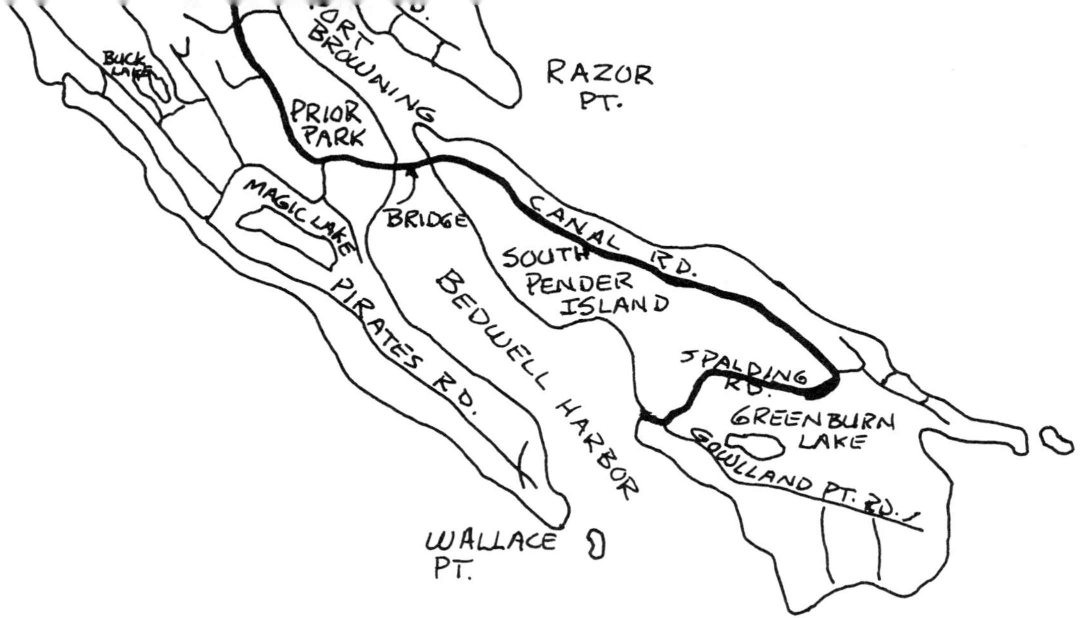
RAZOR PT.
ORT BROWNING
PRIOR PARK
BRIDGE
MAGIC LAKE
CANAL RD.
SOUTH PENDER ISLAND
BEDWELL HARBOR
PIRATES RD.
SPALDING RD.
GREENBURN LAKE
GOWLLAND PT. RD.
WALLACE PT.

North and South Pender Islands

Distance: 34 miles
Terrain: Moderate with long, *steep* hill down to Bedwell Harbor

Pender Island is unique in that a canal separates North Pender from South Pender. A scenic bridge, constructed in 1955, joins the two islands. From this bridge you can view both Bedwell Harbor and Browning Harbor. Below is Mortimer Spit, a popular place for sunning and swimming.

The Canadian customs office is located at Bedwell Harbor Resort, one of the first large-scale marinas to be opened in the islands. During the summer months, several thousand vessels pass through customs every month at this island station.

Pender Island is named after an English sailor, Dan Pender, who served aboard the H.M.S. *Plumper* in 1857. North and South Pender Island covers some 9 square miles and has a population of approximately 1,000 permanent residents. The majority of island residents live on North Pender. Less than 10 percent of the population resides on South Pender. Between these two islands, you will discover many picturesque harbors and beaches worth exploring.

The road from the ferry terminal at Otter Bay (Otter Bay Road) leads to Port Washington. The quaint general store at Port Washington stands at the once bustling ferry harbor of Port Washington. It was built in 1911 and is named after Washington Grimmer, a longtime island farmer and early pioneer.

Accommodations

*A licensed facility serves alcoholic beverages.

Bedwell Harbor Resort* is a modern resort oriented toward boaters, with housekeeping cottages, rooms, general store, dining room, pub, swimming pool and ice cream shop. Shower and laundry facilities are available. Phone: South Pender (604) 629-3212.

Pender Lodge* has quaint cabins and rooms with majestic views of Saltspring Island and the ferries in Swanson Channel. The lodge has a licensed lounge and dining room, swimming pool and tennis courts. Phone: (604) 629-3321.

Roseland Resort, located at the end of South Otter Bay Road, has cottages overlooking Swanson Channel and Otter Bay.

Campgrounds

Prior Park campground has a small number of campsites with fire pits and picnic tables. Well water is available, as are pit toilets.

Your Route

0.0	Ferry terminal at Otter Bay—**straight ahead**
0.4	Otter Bay Road intersection—**turn left**
1.5	Intersection of Otter Bay Road and Port Washington Road—**turn left**

1.7	Port Washington—wharf and small grocery store
3.8	Hope Bay via Port Washington Road
4.9	Driftwood Center (Sandy's Restaurant and Deli) via Bedwell Harbor Road
5.3	Browning Harbor Marina—**turn left**—dining, pub, swimming and possible tent camping
6.5	Prior Park
6.8	Junction to South Pender—**bear right** for Magic Lake area
7.0	P.J. General Store Limited
8.3	Magic Lake—returning to the junction leading to South Pender
9.8	Junction to South Pender—**turn right**
10.4	Bridge connecting North and South Pender
10.6	Public beach access on left
15.9	Bedwell Harbor
16.1	Intersection of Spaulding Road and Gowland Point Road (gravel)—**turn right**
18.0	Gowland Point
20.0	Intersection of Gowland Point Road and Spaulding Road—**turn right**
20.9	Boundary Pass Drive intersection (gravel) leading to public beach access—**turn right**
21.7	Beach
27.5	Junction to North Pender
30.0	Intersection to South Otter Bay Road (gravel) via Bedwell Harbor Road—**turn left**
31.2	Roseland Resort
32.4	Junction of South Otter Bay Road and Otter Bay Road
33.7	Ferry terminal at Otter Bay

GALIANO ISLAND

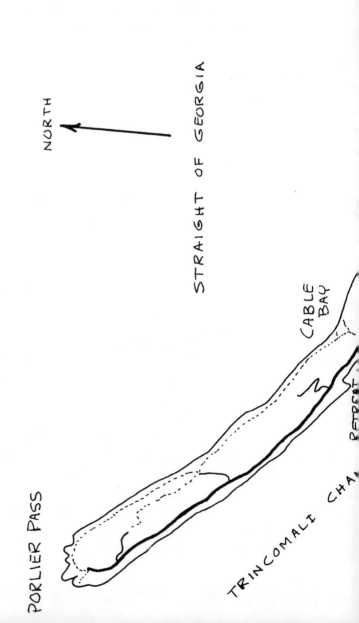

NORTH

STRAIGHT OF GEORGIA

PORLIER PASS

CABLE BAY

TRINCOMALI CHAN

RETREAT

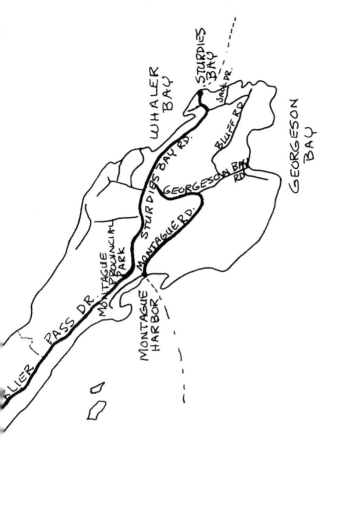

ACTIVE PASS

Galiano Island

Distance: 43 miles
Terrain: Moderate, with several *steep* hills

Galiano Island is named after Dionisio A. Galiano of the Spanish navy, who commanded the exploring vessel *Sutil* in 1772. The island is perhaps best known for its mushroom rock formations.

Galiano Island is 18 miles or so long, and from 1-2 miles in width. The northern end of Galiano joins with Valdes Island to form Porlier Pass. Its southern end joins with Mayne Island to form Active Pass. Galiano also forms an eastern breakwater for Saltspring Island. Approximately 24 inches of rain fall on this dry island in an average year. The island itself slopes toward the Gulf of Georgia on its eastern shore. On this outer eastern edge of the Gulf Islands you will find few bays. On its western side, however, you will find scenic bluffs with superb views toward Saltspring Island and some of the smaller uninhabited Gulf Islands. Approximately 500 residents live year-round on this most scenic island.

July First is the big day on Galiano, when the islanders celebrate Canada Day Jamboree at the North Community Hall on Porlier Pass Drive. The island's public market for local farmers and artisans is located next to the South Community Hall on Sturdies Bay and is open on Fridays from 9:30 a.m. to 12:30 p.m.

The main shopping area on Sturdies Bay has a liquor store, gas station, post office and grocery store. Other stores can be found on Sturdies Bay Road, Porlier Pass Drive, Montague Harbor Marina, and North Galiano.

The Galiano Island Golf and Country Club operates an attractive nine-hole golf course situated off Ellis Road. The course is open to the public.

Island visitors and residents disembark from the mainland ferry at Sturdies Bay. As you leave the ferry, if you pedal up from the terminal and turn left on Burrill Road, bearing right to Bluff Drive, you can enjoy the scenic beauty of Active Pass.

A second ferry wharf on Galiano Island is located at Montague Harbor, where the inter-island ferry to Swartz Bay on Vancouver Island calls.

The main route down the island is Porlier Pass Drive. Shortly after pedaling onto Porlier Pass Drive, you will come to a high point above Montague Harbor where power lines cross the road. Campsites are available at Montague Harbor Park. Many fine views can be had from the western bluffs. Watch for eagles. Beyond the road to Retreat Cove, the road generally drops and descends to sea level at North Galiano.

Accommodations

*A licensed facility serves alcoholic beverages.

Bodega Resort, Ltd., off Porlier Pass Drive, has cottages and is open the year around. Phone: (604) 539-2677.

Galiano Lodge is located just beyond the Sturdies Bay ferry terminal. The lodge offers rooms and cottages overlooking Sturdies Bay and the ferry terminal. A swimming pool and dining room are available. The meals are very good. Expect to be awakened bright and early by ferry whistles and fog horns.

Madrona Lodge may be reached off Porlier Pass Road. Fully equipped housekeeping cottages with fireplaces are available. Phone: (604) 539-2926.

Penny's Cottages overlook Active Pass and are reached off Bluff Road. Phone: (604) 539-5457.

Salishan Resort, on Porlier Pass Road, has housekeeping cottages. Phone: (604) 539-2689.

We haven't made special mention of restaurants, but here is an exception.

The Pink Geranium is a must for a delightful experience in dining that you will long remember. Reservations are necessary. Phone: (604) 539-2477.

Campgrounds

Bellhouse Park is a lovely little day park at the end of Jack Road off Burrill Road—a great place to eat your lunch. The park is located at the eastern entrance to Active Pass and looks out on the lighthouse on Mayne Island. Huge moss-covered slab rocks slope downward toward a rocky beach.

Bluff Park is located off Bluff Road approximately one mile up a very rough gravel road beyond Penny's Cottages. The road winds through beautiful old forests of Douglas fir and cedar trees. The very hearty cyclist (we warned you) will be rewarded with a spectacular view of Active Pass, Pender Island, Saltspring Island and Swartz Bay on Vancouver Island.

Coon Bay—Race Point Area is located at the northern tip of Galiano and is what we consider the prettiest spot on the island. Don't let the jeep road stop you—it's well worth the effort. A series of fingerpoints extend into Porlier Pass, and between these rugged points you'll find sheltered beaches and coves containing many unusual rock formations. You can hike to the lighthouse at Race Point by following a trail along the cliffs overlooking Porlier Pass and Valdes Island. Tent sites are primitive, with no water supply. This is a popular fishing area, and it might be possible to ask one of the motorists to drop off a water supply for you.

Montague Harbor Provincial Park is said to be the most popular marine park in the Gulf Islands. Located at the end of Montague Road, the park is heavily used by bikers, boaters and backpackers. In fact, the 32 sites go very quickly. Water and pit toilet facilities are readily accessible to all sites in the park. If you have a choice, don't pick a campsite near the water pumps unless you want to be lulled to sleep by the squeak of the pump or awakened by the early riser pumping water.

Your Route

0.0   Ferry terminal at Sturdies Bay—**straight ahead**

0.2   Intersection of Burrill Road—**turn left**

0.5   Intersection of Jack Road—**turn left**

0.9   Bellhouse Park

1.3   Burrill Road—**turn left**

3.2   Bluff Park. Return to junction of Burrill Road and Sturdies Bay Road.

5.8   Intersection of Burrill Road and Sturdies Bay Road—**turn left**

7.2   Intersection of Sturdies Bay Road and Georgeson Bay Road—**turn left**

8.0	Intersection of Montague Road—**turn right**
10.6	Montague Provincial Park
14.0	Intersection of Georgeson Bay Road and Porlier Pass Drive—**turn left**
17.5	Intersection of Ganner Drive on left
21.8	Intersection to Retreat Cove on left—very unusual rock formations
23.9	Viewpoints and park on left
25.9	Cook Road on right leads to Coon Point—3 miles over a very rough gravel and dirt road
27.7	Spanish Hills store (watch the sea lions play)
43.0	Ferry terminal at Sturdies Bay

MAYNE ISLAND

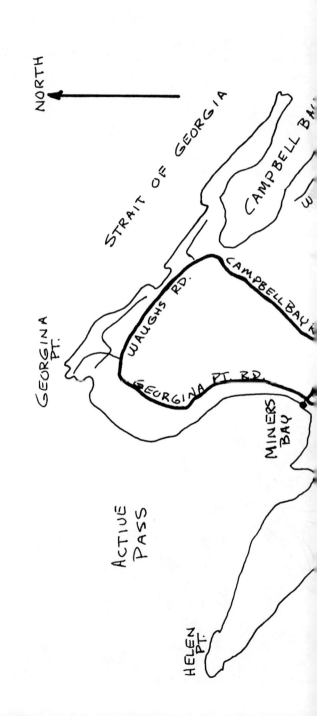

NORTH

STRAIT OF GEORGIA

CAMPBELL BAY

GEORGINA PT.

WAUGHS RD.

CAMPBELL BAY R

GEORGINA PT. RD.

MINERS BAY

ACTIVE PASS

HELEN PT.

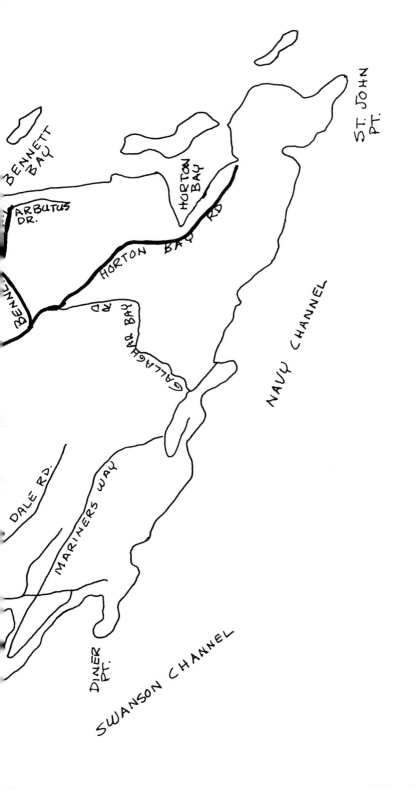

Mayne Island

Distance: 20 miles
Terrain: Moderate to hilly

Mayne Island covers 8 square miles and is approximately 5 miles long and 3 miles wide. Over 560 residents live on this island on a permanent basis.

Mayne Island was named after Lt. Charles Mayne of the British navy, who served aboard the H.M.S. *Plumper* when the Gulf Islands were surveyed in the late 1850s.

Village Bay is the site of the present ferry terminal; however, the Miner's Bay area, known to oldtimers as "The Pass," has always been the hub of the island's activities. During the 1858 Fraser River Gold Rush, Mayne Island's Miner's Bay was a favorite stopover for miners bound from Victoria to the mainland. Shortly after the island was settled, a post office and general store were built at Miner's Bay. Residents of Pender Island, Saturna Island and Galiano Island rowed their boats to Mayne Island to collect their mail. For over 80 years, the Mayne Island residents gathered at The Pass on mailboat days to exchange news and wait for the mail.

There are two old hotels on Mayne. Springwater Lodge, built on the site of the islands' first post office, has served the traveling public continuously longer than any other in the province. From the hotel there is an excellent view of Miner's Bay and the marine traffic in Active Pass. Mayne Inn

is an old two-story hotel opened in the early 1900s for

employees of a brickworks plant. The plant was only partially finished, as a result of the First World War, and the inn stood idle until the Second World War when it was reopened as the Hollandia Hotel, in 1942. The name was changed to Mayne Inn in 1968. It offers a warm, friendly atmosphere with an eclectic decor. The dining room, above an outside deck, overlooks the spacious grounds extending down to a weathered dock. After a hard day's ride, you can relax on the deck with a tall cool drink, or in case of bad weather you can sink into an old leather couch before their large stone fireplace and warm your feet.

The lighthouse at Georgina Point was built in 1885 and is open to the public from 1:00 p.m. to 3:00 p.m. daily.

Accommodations

*A licensed facility serves alcoholic beverages.

Blue Vista Resort, at Bennett Bay on Arbutus Drive, provides housekeeping rooms. Phone: (604) 539-2463.

Marisol Village Cottages, on Wilks Road near Bennett Bay, has housekeeping cottages. Phone: (604) 539-2336.

Mayne Inn, * at Bennett Bay, is a fully equipped hotel with dining room and lounge. Rooms are clean, with central bath facilities. Phone: (604) 539-2632. (At the time of this printing, the hotel has been closed.)

Springwater Lodge, * on Miner's Bay, has rooms with central bathroom facilities, a dining room and pub. Phone: (604) 539-5521.

Campgrounds

There are no public campgrounds on Mayne Island.

Your Route

0.0	Ferry terminal at Village Bay—**straight ahead** up the hill on Village Bay Road
1.5	Miner's Bay Trading Post (general store)—**turn left** toward Miner's Bay

1.6	Springwater Lodge and Government Wharf—**turn** onto Georgina Point Road
3.2	Georgina Point—**turn left** to lighthouse
3.5	Georgina Point Lighthouse
3.8	Intersection of Georgina Point Road and Waughs Road
4.6	Porter Road on left

4.8	Campbell Bay Road (gravel)
6.4	Intersection of Campbell Bay Road and Fernhill Road—**turn left**
7.2	Mayne Island Center Store
7.3	Junction Horton Bay Road and Bennett Bay Road—**continue on** Bennett Bay Road
7.4	Fernhill Herb Farm Bed & Breakfast
8.4	Mayne Inn
8.9	Blue Vista Resort on Arbutus Drive
9.0	End of road
9.6	Mayne Inn
10.7	Horton Bay Road (gravel)
11.1	Gallagher Bay Road on right—continue **straight ahead**
13.0	End of Horton Bay Road
14.9	Junction Horton Bay Road and Gallagher Bay Road—**turn left** onto Gallagher Bay Road
16.3	Piggott Bay
16.5	Gallagher Bay Road and Marine Drive
18.5	Dalton Drive and Dinner Bay Road
19.1	End of Dinner Bay Road—private beach
19.7	Dalton Drive
20.2	Ferry terminal

SATURNA ISLAND

NORTH

STRAIT OF GEORGIA

WINTER COVE

WINTER COVE RD

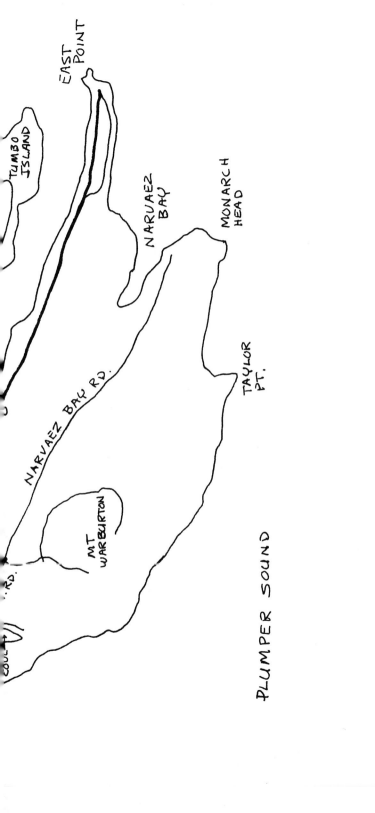

EAST POINT

TUMBO ISLAND

NARVAEZ BAY

MONARCH HEAD

NARVAEZ BAY RD.

TAYLOR PT.

MT WARBURTON

RD.

PLUMPER SOUND

Chapter 6

Saturna Island

Distance: 21 miles
**Terrain: Moderately hilly with several *steep*
  hills**

Saturna island is named after the Spanish naval schooner
Saturina. The ship was commanded by Captain Jose Maria
Narvaez in 1791, on its exploratory cruise through the Straits
of Juan de Fuca.

Saturna is the easternmost island in the Gulf Island group.
It is the least developed of all the Gulf Islands as a result of
its distance from the ports of Vancouver and Victoria and
its mountainous character. Although Saturna Island is larger
than Mayne and nearly the size of Pender, it has the smallest

population and the most untouched landscape. This 12-square-mile island is also the most difficult to reach. Getting on or off Saturna can be a chore since the ferry does not run as often as the other island ferries. Also, it is necessary to transfer ferries at Village Bay on Mayne Island.

Lyall Harbor is the Saturna ferry terminal and the focal point of the island's population of 230 inhabitants. Island residents enjoy their isolation, and self-sufficiency is a way of life on the island. The general store, post office and pub are located at the ferry terminal.

The island has no overnight camping facilities. The 300-acre Winter Cove Marine Park has picnic tables and fire

The famous Saturna Lamb Barbecue occurs on the first weekend in July of each year. This tradition began in 1949 when a group of islanders gathered to barbecue a few lambs. Today, as many as 30 or more lambs are roasted over open pits, and 1,500 or more people travel to the island for this annual feast. Other than the lamb barbecue, few activities take place on the island.

After leaving the ferry terminal via East Point Road, you soon come upon the Saturna General Store, located at the intersection of East Point and Narvaez Bay Roads. At this junction you descend rapidly into the valley at the head of Lyall Harbor. East Point Road climbs very steeply out of the valley and eventually meets Winter Cove Road which leads into Winter Cove Marine Park.

Winter Cove is very picturesque, and it is worthwhile spending some time here. Hike through the park along a well kept trail to Winter Point. Here you can have lunch on the rocks, bask in the sun and watch the boats attempt to enter Winter Cove through Boat Passage. Because of the strong current, some make it and some don't. Across Boat Passage from Winter Point is Samuel Island.

The route from Winter Cove to East Point follows the eastern shore of the island and provides splendid views of Georgia Strait, Cabbage Island and Tumbo Island. Much of the road is gravel but not too rough. At the end of the road you will come upon the East Point Lighthouse, built in 1888. Spend some time exploring the unusual sandstone rock formations and bluffs. At low tide you can walk around East Point and photograph the bluffs and lighthouse from water level.

Accommodations

*A licensed facility serves alcoholic beverages.

Boot Cove Lodge is located at the end of Boot Cove Road and has the only overnight accommodations on Saturna Island. The lodge provides rooms and home cooked meals. Phone: (604) 539-2254.

Lighthouse Pub* provides the only food service on the island, but may not be open on Sunday.

Winter Cove Marine Park contains several picnic tables, fire pits and a hand-pumped well. Should you pitch your tent, park personnel will ask that you promptly remove it.

Campgrounds

There are no overnight public campgrounds on Saturna Island.

Your Route

0.0	Ferry terminal—**straight ahead** up East Point Road
0.2	Boot Cove—road on **right**
1.0	Junction*—Saturna General Store—**turn left** and continue on East Point Road down steep hill
1.7	Sunset Boulevard—on left leading to Lyall Harbor Beach
2.0	Lyall Harbor Beach
2.3	Back to East Point Road—**turn left** and climb steep hill
3.7	Junction of Winter Cove and East Point Road—**turn left** on gravel road leading to Winter Cove Park
4.0	Winter Cove Park
4.3	Junction of Winter Cove Road and East Point Road—**straight ahead** on gravel road (portions asphalt) to East Point Lighthouse; East Point Road turns into Tumbo Channel Road
10.9	East Point Lighthouse
11.0	Cliffside Road on left—**turn left** onto Cliffside Road
12.6	Back to main road (Tumbo Channel Road)—**turn left**
17.6	Junction of Winter Cove Road—leading to Winter Cove Park and East Point Road
19.6	Junction and General Store—**turn right**
20.6	Ferry terminal

*Narvaez Bay Road at the junction is a gravel road dead-ending at Narvaez Bay (3.9 miles). The gravel road leading to Mount Warburton Pike is *very* rough and steep. At 2.8 miles, the one-lane road ends at the radio facility. The view is breathtaking as you look out over the islands and the green meadows falling off toward the shoreline.

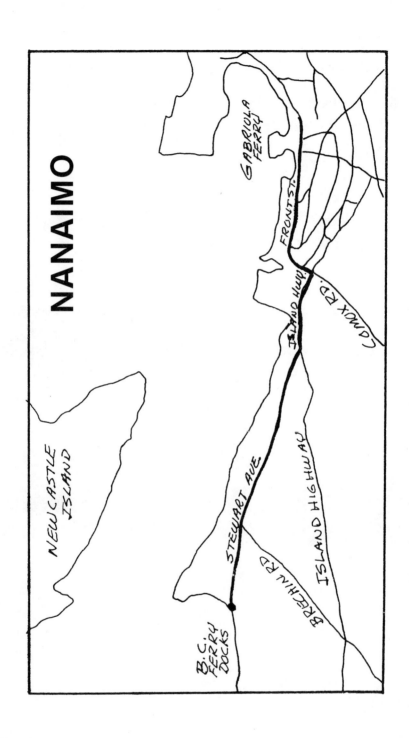

NANAIMO

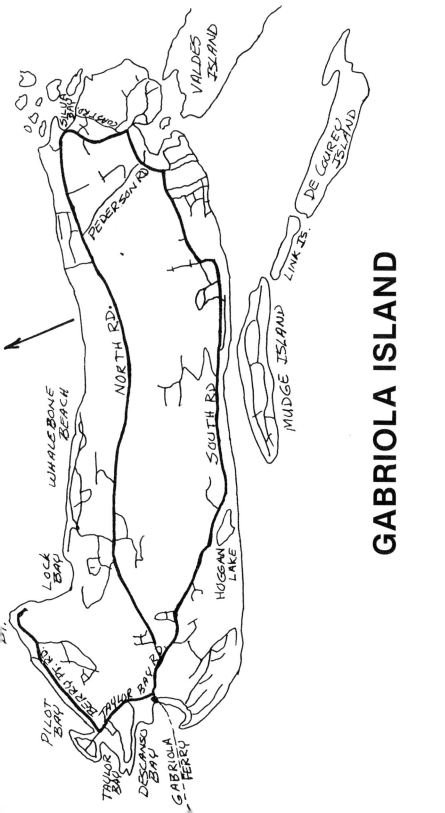

GABRIOLA ISLAND

Gabriola Island

Distance: 31 miles
Terrain: Moderate

    Gabriola Island is small—11 miles long and 2 miles across at its widest point. Located approximately 3 miles off the eastern coast of Vancouver Island and slightly south of the city of Nanaimo, some people consider it to be a part of the rural community of this expanding hub city (pop. 50,000). Many others consider Gabriola to be one of the Gulf Islands.

Gabriola Island has excellent ferry service and is reached via a 20-minute ferry ride. The Gabriola ferry departs from a small terminal in South Nanaimo approximately 2½ miles south of the main B.C. ferry terminal in Nanaimo's Departure Bay, where the ferry from Horseshoe Bay docks. The B.C. ferry leaves every hour on the hour from North Vancouver's Horseshoe Bay for Nanaimo, and takes 1½ hours to make the 30-mile crossing.

Gabriola was explored by the Spanish naval explorers Galiano and Valdez. In 1792 they anchored their schooners, the *Sutil* and the *Mexicana,* in Descanso Bay, the site of the present Gabriola ferry terminal, for repairs. The two officers explored the shoreline of the bay and adjacent waters where Galiano discovered unusual rock formations which he named after himself. This attraction looks like a tidal wave frozen in stone and is approximately 300 feet long and 12 feet high. Today this site is called the Malaspina Galleries. The Galleries are reached from a winding footpath at the end of Malaspina Drive.

Gabriola is often called the petroglyph island, due to the large number of Indian rock carvings found here. The petroglyph site is in a large secluded clearing covered with scattered flat stones, small to huge in size, many overgrown with vegetation. For those of you interested in native Indian culture, imagine the excitement of pulling back old moss to discover ancient stone carvings! To reach the site, locate the United Church at Degnen Bay and follow the fence along a dirt road behind the church a few hundred feet to a clearing among the trees on the left. The site, originally privately owned, was generously deeded to the Crown, and is now part of a tree farm license. Protecting these petroglyphs from acts of vandalism such as has occurred at the Malaspina Galleries should be of concern to everyone.

Accommodations

*A licensed facility serves alcoholic beverages.

Haven-By-the-Sea* is a year-round resort and conference center on Davis Road, minutes from the ferry. Dining and dancing in a relaxed atmosphere. Phone: (604) 247-9231.

Silva Bay Boatel & Resort, at Silva Bay, is approximately 11 miles from the ferry. A wide variety of services and facilities are available. Phone: (604) 247-9351; 247-9267.

Surf Lodge* is a beautiful, rustic log lodge with a massive stone fireplace, located on the shore of Clarke Bay on Berry Point Road. Comfortable rooms are available in the main lodge or in individual private cabins. The lodge has a saltwater pool, tennis courts, dining room (homestyle cooking) and a pub. Phone: (604) 247-9231.

The Grand Hotel, at the south end of the island, overlooks the ocean and is situated on cliffs several hundred feet above the water. A neat place for a snack and friendly chat with the owners. Phone: (604) 247-9303.

Twin Beaches, on Taylor Bay, minutes from the ferry, has rental cottages for rent by the week or month. Phone: (604) 247-8518.

Campgrounds

Gabriola Island has several provincial parks and beaches; however, there are no public overnight camping facilities. Only B.C. Credit Union members are allowed to camp on 30 acres of land owned by Nanaimo Housing Services Corporation, Ltd. This acreage is located off Taylor Bay, near the B & K Shopping Center.

Gabriola Sands Provincial Park, for day use, is located between Taylor Bay and Pilot Bay—a very short ride from the B & K Shopping Center.

Your Route

0.0	Main B.C. Ferry terminal in Nanaimo's Departure Bay. **Straight ahead** on Stewart Avenue. Stewart Avenue **(stay left)** intersects with and becomes Island Highway (Terminal Avenue). Be advised to remain on the left to enter the left-turn

	lane, and **turn left** on Comox Road, which feeds into Front Street. Front Street will lead you to the Gabriola ferry terminal.
2.6	Gabriola ferry terminal in South Nanaimo
2.6	Ferry terminal on Gabriola Island (Descanso Bay)—**straight ahead**
2.8	Taylor Bay Road on left—**turn left**
3.8	Malaspina Drive—**turn left**
4.5	Malaspina Galleries
5.2	Back to Taylor Bay Road
5.3	Davis Road—**turn left**
5.6	Haven-By-The-Sea Resort
5.9	Back to Taylor Bay Road—**turn left** and continue on Taylor Bay Road, which leads into Berry Point Road
6.1	B & K Shopping Center on Berry Point Road, where you can buy lunch items
7.1	Surf Lodge on right
7.8	End of Berry Point Road
10.8	Intersection of Taylor Bay Road and North Road—**turn left** on North Road
11.1	Intersection of North Road and South Road—**bear left** and continue on North Road past Peterson Road
17.6	Gravel Road on **left** leading to Grand Hotel
17.9	Grand Hotel
18.2	Back to Main Road—**turn left**
19.2	Silva Bay—return to Main Road, **turn left** and continue on
22.0	United Church—site of petroglyphs behind church (white church on right)
24.7	Fern Road on right—old brickyard works on left
25.4	Top of big hill

27.9	Junction of South Road and North Road—**turn left**
28.4	Ferry terminal on Gabriola
28.4	Gabriola ferry terminal—South Nanaimo
31.0	B.C. Ferry terminal on Departure Bay

Your Bicycle and Gear

Bicycling in the Gulf Islands, like bicycling anywhere, can be very enjoyable, provided, of course, that you are prepared for your adventure and have no mechanical breakdowns. How can you prevent mechanical breakdowns? The answer to this question can be found in two simple words—preventive maintenance!

Before you leave home, be certain that your bicycle and equipment are in good operating condition. In the Gulf Islands, you will be biking in remote areas, on hard-surfaced roads and on gravel roads. Service facilities, if available at all, are at best sparse. Your bicycle should have good tires, and you will want to carry patch material and the necessary tools for repairing flat tires.

We don't encourage riding your bicycle at night, for safety reasons. However, we do recommend that your bicycle be equipped with lights, because bike touring can be unpredictable and you don't want to be caught without a good lighting system. We prefer a generator-operated headlight and red taillight. Also, you may want to consider a flashlight with a red filter to be mounted on the rear of your bicycle because when you stop, so does your generator. Being without lights, especially your red rear-warning light, is not a good position to be in on a dark, narrow road. We also recommend a good-fitting lightweight helmet for head protection.

With your bicycle in good operating condition, and the necessary tools on hand to repair breakdowns, all that remains to check out is your equipment. Everyone has their ɔwn ideas of what is proper and adequate. With experience, you will soon learn to choose lightweight gear. Our purpose ɪs not to say what one must have, but we can share with you ɪow *we* are equipped. For *your* adventure, you can then do your own thing.

Our bicycles are equipped with rear panniers; front panniers; seat bag for tools, tire patch material, tape, cleaning ɪag, and other miscellaneous necessities; handlebar bag for ɪrail mix, other goodies, maps, wallet, etc.; grab-on handlebar ɔads; water bottle with alloy cage; and thumb-lock pump. Ɔn the rear carrier we place a lightweight down sleeping ɔag, inserted in a large plastic bag for rain protection, and ɪ therm-a-rest mattress. The tent—a 2-person Mt. McKinley with rain fly—is mounted under the bar between the seat and ɪhe handlebars. The night lantern—a Coleman white gas (peak one)—provides 125-candle power for those late-evening ɪinners by candlelight. The lantern also comes in handy for ɪlean-up and late-night tent erection.

Food Suggestions and Cooking Equipment

What you eat on your tour depends on how much weight you want to carry, how far you can comfortably ride between your known sources of supplies, and what your budget allows. Unlike backpacking in the wilderness, there are a number of options to choose from on your tour. You can pack the food in on your bike, buy it as you travel along, rely on restaurants, or do some combination of the above. To help you develop your own style of food preparation, we would like to share some of our own food planning ideas. We also highly recommend reading books on backpacking recipes and hints, such as *The Well Fed Backpacker,* by June Fleming, or *The Outdoor Epicure,* published by R.E.I. Co-op, Inc.

When we began our touring, we found the problem of what to take for food to be quite a challenge. We tried different suggestions, such as frozen meat securely wrapped in layers of plastic and paper, then tucked inside a sleeping bag. The meat is well insulated and *will* stay fresh for hours in the hot sun. Unfortunately, you may wind up sleeping on miserable wet spots from the package condensation.

Pedaling light, with all freeze-dried foods—another suggestion we tried—proved to be quite expensive and a culinary disaster at the campsite. We recommend trying out dried foods gradually to learn which ones are acceptable to you. Our method is to mix a few basic freeze-dried items with grocery store foods. Be creative, scout the supermarket shelves for nutritious quick-fix lightweight nonperishable items. You can add freeze-dried chopped chicken, pork or vegetables to packaged rice or noodle mixes in flavored sauces. Curry powder, raisins and fresh ginger add extra zest.

One of our dinner favorites is Japanese noodle-soup mix (saimin) with pork or chicken and vegetables, topped with chopped fresh green onions. For dessert, add water to premeasured dried skim milk and instant pudding.

Lunches can be cheese or salami sandwiches, apples, potato chips and inexpensive packets of dried vegetable juice. Small-sized bread mashes up less, and we count out only what slices will be used.

Breakfasts are usually light, with toasted English muffins spread with our homemade blackberry jam, coffee, and cut-up fresh fruit with a healthy squeeze of fresh lime. On occasion, we might have packets of instant oatmeal to which can be added raisins, granola, and dried skim milk powder. Just add hot water for an easy breakfast mix. Freeze-dried scrambled eggs with canned ham added is also an acceptable variation.

On longer rides, several smaller meals spaced throughout the day maintain body energy better than three larger meals. Take only what foods you'll need, and do any necessary premixing, measuring or packaging at home. Remember to plan well so that the choice of foods is coordinated with the pots and number of burners being carried. It can be quite frustrating if you run short of the right-size pots needed for a particular food, or if you are trying to juggle a three-pot dinner on one burner while the cooked foods are getting cold.

Even if you choose to eat at restaurants, we recommend carrying at least one emergency meal in case you are stranded.

Trail mix, candy bars and dried fruits make good snack foods for quick energy, but remember that foods with high carbohydrates provide short-lasting nourishment. Foods greater in proteins and fats will provide longer-term energy boosts. These include cheeses, nuts, beef jerky and yogurt, if available. On the other hand, some of us would never make it to the top of a murderous hill without the reward of a candy treat!

The cooking equipment carried consists of a lightweight mountaineering white-gas Primus, and whatever pots and pans are required to prepare the planned menu. An extra water container is carried, as well as a reserve bottle of white gas for the few occasions when the stove or lantern runs dry.

Your Clothes and Miscellaneous

Clothes are a personal thing. There are, however, a number of items you may want to consider—like your bathing suit, for that occasional dip in the ocean or the evening dip in the lake. Don't forget your lightweight rain gear either, as you may experience an occasional heavy Canadian mist in the form of rain.

Wool, or polypropylene with wool, is an item every biker should consider—wool pants, sweaters, hat, gloves and stockings. We cannot say enough about the merits of wool. With wool, you will normally always remain warm except in the most adverse conditions. Even then, wool will keep you warmer and dryer than those garments without it.

Wearing layered clothing, so you can remove your outer garments as the day becomes warmer, is a good plan. Some kind of leather shoes will keep your feet warmer than wet tennis shoes, should you be caught in a cold rain.

A small first-aid kit is a necessity, as are extra flashlight bulbs, batteries and waterproof matches.

Thinking Metric

Canada is on the metric system. Many visitors from the United Stated may find the metric system confusing, but it needn't be this way.

The first place you are exposed to the metric system is on the highway: "100" doesn't invite you to speed down the highway; it means 100 kilometers, or 62.14 mph. One kilometer (km) equals 0.6214 miles. For quick mental arithmetic, we can use a conversion factor of 60 percent and estimate miles or miles per hour fairly accurately:

$$30 \text{ km} \times .60 = 18 \text{ miles/mph}$$
$$40 \text{ km} \times .60 = 24 \text{ miles/mph}$$
$$50 \text{ km} \times .60 = 30 \text{ miles/mph}$$
$$60 \text{ km} \times .60 = 36 \text{ miles/mph}$$
$$70 \text{ km} \times .60 = 42 \text{ miles/mph}$$
$$80 \text{ km} \times .60 = 48 \text{ miles/mph}$$

Canadian gasoline is sold by the liter. One liter equals 1.0567 quarts (actually, a liter is 5 percent larger than a quart). We all know that there are four quarts to the gallon. It takes only 3.785 liters to fill a gallon crock but, for our purposes you can figure a liter is approximately a quarter of a gallon or one quart.

The formula for converting Celsius temperatures to Fahrenheit is:

$$(\text{Celsius} \times 9/5) + 32 = \text{Fahrenheit}$$

As the formula tells us, if we know a temperature in Celsius we multiply degrees Celsius times 9/5 and add 32, since the Celsius scale starts out 32 degrees lower. Fortunately, you can make a reasonably accurate conversion in your head